Oracle Database For People Who Has No Time

Table of Contents

Chapter 1- Introduction

A database is a collection of data/information. A Database Management System (DBMS) is a collection of programs that have been written to manage a database. A DBMS acts as an interface between a user and a database. A DBMS that works based on the relational model is referred to as a Relational Database Management System (RDBMS).

Oracle is an Object-Relational DBMS and the leading vendor in the world. Almost half of all RDBMS available worldwide are owned by Oracle. The Oracle database is produced and marketed by the Oracle Corporation. It is the largest software company in the database business field.

Every Oracle Database is made up of Logical and Physical Structures. The Logical Structures are the tablespaces, extents, schema objects and segments. The Physical Structures are the Datafiles, Control File and Redo Log Files.

A databases is divided into tablespaces, which are logical storage units. The purpose of tablespaces is to group logically-related structures together. Each tablespace has one of more datafiles.

The Oracle Database can run on the major platforms, including UNIX, Windows, Linux and Mac OS. The database comes in different versions. You should choose the version you need based on your requirements and budget. The Oracle Database editions are hierarchically organized as follows:

1. Enterprise Edition

   This edition provides all the features, including superior security and performance, and it is the most robust Oracle

Database Edition.

2. Standard Edition

It provides users with base functionality. It is suitable for users who do not need the robust features provided by the Enterprise Edition.

3. Express Edition (XE)

This is a free, lightweight and limited Linux and Windows edition. It is easy and fast to install.

4. Oracle Lite

This edition runs on mobile devices.

As stated earlier, the architecture is split between Logical Structure and Physical Structure. For grid computing/large-scale distributed computing, the location of data is irrelevant and transparent to the user. This allows for a more modular physical structure that can be modified without affecting the database activity, users or the data. This way of resource sharing allows for flexible data networks whose capacity can be scaled up or down to suit demand, with no degradation of service. It also means that there is no single point whose failure can bring the database down.

Chapter 2- Who is it for?

First and foremost, this book is dedicated to the managers who have no background in database technologies yet have to manage the DBAs. Due to explosion in the data-related technologies such as Big Data, Data Mining etc., managers are finding that they are increasingly getting closer to the DBAs and vice versa. Without fully understanding the database technology, they are bound to make mistakes.

Secondly, this book is also dedicated to the developers who may not be fully trained in the Oracle Database technology but have to develop applications with it. As above, without fully understanding the technology, the application will end up in a disaster.

Finally, this book is dedicated to DBAs who have to communicate or work with everyone else on a daily basis. The DBAs have to explain to them every words that they speak and yet knowing full well that the colleagues may not fully understand everything that has been explained to them.

This is the best book for you that will help you grasp every aspect of Oracle 12c database. The author has written the book in a step-by-step approach while adding explanations to every step. Enjoy reading!

Chapter 3- Introduction to Database Technology in General

A database is stored in a database management system (DBMS). The DBMS is a system software that facilitates the creation and management of databases. It provides programmers and users with a systematic way to create, update, retrieve and manage data.

With a DBMS, end users are able to create, update, read and delete data from a database. The DBMS acts as an interface between the database and application programs/end users. Let us discuss the three DMBSs that are commonly used in the world:

MS SQL Server

Microsoft SQL Server is a relational database management system (RDBMS) capable of supporting a wide variety of transaction processing, analytics applications and business intelligence in corporate IT environments. By relation we mean that the database is made of the major components of a relational model which are Tables, Records/Tuples, Fields and Columns/Attributes. MS SQL Server is one of the leading database technologies in the world. MS SQL Server is developed by Microsoft as its name suggests.

Just like the other RDBMSs, MS SQL Server is built on top of SQL (Structured Query Language) which is a standardized programming language used by IT professionals like Database Administrators (DBAs) to manage databases and query the data they contain. MS SQL Server is also tied to Transact-SQL (T-SQL), which is an advanced implementation of SQL from Microsoft adding proprietary programming extensions to the standard language, that is, SQL.

Microsoft released SQL Server 2017 on October 2, 2017, and this version is capable of running on a number of Linux distributions.

Oracle

Oracle database is an object-relational database management system developed and marketed by the Oracle Corporation. It was developed in 1977 by Lawrence Ellison together with other developers. Today, Oracle is one of the most-trusted database engines in the world.

In Oracle, users and application front ends may access the data objects via SQL. The Oracle database architecture is fully scalable and highly used by global enterprises that normally manage and process data across local and wide area networks. Oracle database comes with its own network component that allows communications to be done across networks. The Oracle database has outdone MS SQL Server in the corporate database market.

The Oracle database is capable of running on various platforms, which include Windows, Linux, UNIX and Mac OS.

MySQL

MySQL forms the most popular open source database management system in the world. Some of its features that can be attributed to its popularity include ease-of-use, reliability and performance. It is highly used in the development of web applications. High profile web properties such as Twitter, Facebook, YouTube and the top five websites use MySQL. Some of the capabilities provided by MySQL include full commit, crash recovery, rollback and row-level locking. It also comes with various database drivers and visual tools that help DBAs and developers create and manage business-critical MySQL applications.

Chapter 4: Oracle Database Architecture

The Oracle Database Server is made up of a number of components. Some of the components are memory structures, while others are processes that execute particular tasks behind the scenes. Disk resources are also available in the architecture, and these are used for storing data used by applications to track the entire organization. Special resources are designed to facilitate the recovery of data in case of occurrence of problems such as disk failure and incorrect entry. When all these features work together, they enable Oracle to manage data for applications that range from small "data marts" with less than five users to enterprise-wide client/server applications used for processing online transactions for over 50,000 users in a global environment.

An Oracle Instance is made up of the following components:

- Oracle memory structures.

- Oracle background processes.

- Oracle disk utilization resources.

The above components run together to allow users to read and modify data.

Components of Oracle Architecture

The following are the various components that make up the Oracle architecture:

1. Memory (SGA , PGA)

   Oracle uses memory structures for completion of jobs.

Example, the memory is used for storage of the running program code and the data that is shared amongst users. Oracle has two basic memory structures namely system global area (SGA) and the program global area (PGA).

System Global Area (SGA)

The SGA is a shared memory region that has data and control information for a single Oracle instance. It is the most important memory structure in Oracle. Whenever you hear DBAs talk about memory, they are referring to the SGA. It is allocated on startup and de-allocated on shutdown. To ensure optimal performance, the SGA should be as large as possible to minimize I/O operations and store as much data as possible. Below are the items that make up the SGA:

- Buffer cache.

- Shared pool.

- Redo log buffer.

The buffer cache stores the most recently used blocks of data. This helps in the improvement of performance for subsequent selects and data changes. The shared pool is the portion of SGA with shared memory constructs like shared SQL areas. The shared SQL area is necessary for the processing of every unique SQL statement that is submitted to the database. The redo log buffer stores redo entries, that is, a log of changes that are made to the database. The redo entries that are stored here are normally written to an online redo log file. The redo log file helps when there is a need for database recovery.

Program Global Area (PGA)

The PGA is a memory area that helps the user processes to

execute. The question is, why do the users need their own area in order to execute? The reason is because although the parse information for SQL statements may already be available in the shared area, that is, library cache, the values the user may need to execute the "update" and "search" upon cannot be shared. The PGA is used for storage of real values instead of bind variables for the execution of SQL statements.

Initialization Parameters

Once an Oracle instance is started, it reads the initialization parameters from the initialization parameter file (init.ora). If there are some initialization parameters not included in the initialization parameter file, the database will supply the defaults. The following are the functions of the initialization parameters:

- Set limits for entire database

- Set limits on the database resources

- Set limits for user or processes.

Some of the parameters in the parameter file include the amount of memory allocated to the instance, internal optimization parameters and the file locations. The parameter initialization file may be in the form of a read-only text file or read/write binary file. The binary file is referred to as "server parameter file". It provides a basis for self-tuning by the Oracle Database.

The initialization parameters tell Oracle programs the amount of memory to allocate, where to store files related to the database and where to find the existing data files. Each parameter has a name and the corresponding value. Consider the example parameter given below:

db_cache_size=8192

The parameter tells Oracle the size for each database block, and this is 8192 bytes. You can use the "ALTER SYSTEM" commands to change the initialization parameters and persist changes across a startup or shutdown. Some of the parameters are dynamic and can be changed while the database is running. Example:

SQL> alter system set db_recovery_file_dest_size=15g;

```
SQL> alter system set db_recovery_file_dest_size=15g;
System altered.
SQL>
```

In the above example, we have dynamically changed the value of *db_recovery_file_dest* parameter to 15 gigabytes.

SP File

The Oracle spfile (server parameter file) is a binary representation of the *init.ora* file, which is text-based. The spfile was first introduced in Oracle 9i. The previous versions of Oracle relied on the text based pfile (parameter file) for storage of initialization parameters.

Unlike the pfile, the spfile cannot be edited in a text editor. Instead, we modify it using the "ALTER SYSTEM" command. By default, the spfile is stored at the "$ORACLE_HOME/dbs/spfile[SID].ora" directory, where SID is the instance name.

To know whether your database is using a pfile or spfile, run the following command:

SQL> show parameter spfile

If no rows are returned, pfile is being used. If it returns any value with filename (together with the path), then the current running instance is using spfile:

```
SQL> show parameter spfile;

NAME                                    TYPE          VALUE
--------------------------------------- ------------- --------------------------------
spfile                                  string        /app/centos/product/12.1.0/dbh
                                                      ome_1/dbs/spfileorcl.ora
```

In my case, I am using the spfile.

To create the spfile from pfile, you must be logged in as the SYSDBA. You can then use the "CREATE" command as follows:

Connect system/manager as sysdba;

CREATE SPFILE FROM PFILE;

The command will create the spfile in non-default location, that is, $ORACLE_HOME/database. However, it is possible for you to specify the paths as follows:

**CREATE SPFILE='/u01/admin/prod/pfile/file_mydb.ora'
FROM
PFILE=/u01/admin/prod/pfile/initprod.ora';**

To alter the parameters of the spfile, follow the syntax given below:

**SQL> alter system set [parameter=value] sid='[sid|*]'
scope=[memory|spfile|both];**

The SCOPE clause defines the scope of change for the dynamic and static parameters as described below:

- SPFILE- this allows for dynamic and static parameter changes. The changes will be recorded in the spfile, and they will take effect in the next start.

- Memory- this allows for dynamic parameter changes. Changes will be applied to the memory only.

- BOTH- this allows for dynamic parameter changes. The changes will be applied to both the memory and spfile.

Control File

This is a small binary file in which the physical structure of the database is defined. Every Oracle database has the control file. The control file has the following information:

- Database name

- Timestamp of creation of the database

- Names and locations of the associated redo log files and datafiles.

- Checkpoint information

- Current log sequence number

The control file is created during the creation of the database and it must be available anytime the database is open.

To know the location of Oracle control files, use the following commands:

SQL> show parameter control_files

In my case, I get the following output:

```
SQL> show parameter control_file;

NAME                              TYPE        VALUE
--------------------------------- ----------- ------------------------------
control_file_record_keep_time     integer     7
control_files                     string      /app/centos/oradata/orcl/contr
                                              ol01.ctl, /app/centos/recovery
                                              _area/orcl/control02.ctl
SQL>
```

You can also use the following command:

SQL> database backup controlfile to trace

SCN

The System Change Number (SCN) is a primary way of maintaining data consistency in Oracle database. Oracle uses SCN to control consistency, changing vectors in redo logs and in performing recovery. The SCN may be understood as the Oracle's way of representing time. The SCN is found in both the memory and the disk.

The SCN number has two parts, that is, SCN Base & SCB Wrap, and it is generated on request in response to an event. It has a total of 48 bits (6 bytes). Out of the 48 bits, SCN_WRAP takes 16 bits (2 Bytes) while SCN_BASE takes 32 bits (4 Bytes). Both the BASE & WRAP help in controlling the SCN's increment and in ensuring that the database does not run out of it. For you to see the current SCN number, you should query the V$DATABASE view using the command given below:

SQL> select current_scn from V$database;

The SCN will be shown in the form of a number:

```
SQL> select current_scn from V$database;
CURRENT_SCN
-----------
    2386903
SQL>
```

The following command can help you convert the SCN to a hexadecimal value:

SQL> select to_char('1123790','xxxxxxxx') scn_hex from dual;

```
SQL> select to_char('1123790','xxxxxxxx') scn_hex from dual;
SCN_HEX
--------
   1125ce
```

Try to access the same view again and again and you will get a different value for the SCN.

SQL> select current_scn from V$database;

You will notice that the value of SCN will increase after every query.

```
SQL> select current_scn from U$database;
CURRENT_SCN
-----------
    2387668
SQL> /
CURRENT_SCN
-----------
    2387673
SQL> /
CURRENT_SCN
-----------
    2387674
SQL>
```

You can easily see the two values by querying the user-SMON_SCN_TIME table owned by SYS user. The following command illustrates this:

SQL> select SCN_wrp, SCN_bas, SCN from smon_SCN_time where rownum < 3;

```
SQL> select SCN_wrp, SCN_bas, SCN from smon_SCN_time where rownum < 3;
   SCN_WRP     SCN_BAS        SCN
----------  ----------  ----------
         0       21871      21871
         0      259440     259440
SQL>
```

The table stores the entries for the generated SCNs. It stores data in increments of 3 minutes and holds data worth 5 days. You can count the available number of records by running the following command:

SQL> select count(*) from SMON_SCN_TIME;

```
SQL> select count(*) from SMON_SCN_TIME;
  COUNT(*)
----------
       107
SQL>
```

Tablespaces and Datafiles

In Oracle, tablespaces are logical entities for data storage. The work of tablespaces is to organize data logically.

Oracle stores data physically in *datafiles* which correspond to a tablespace. This means that a tablespace may have one or more datafiles. The datafiles are physical structures conforming to the operating system in which the Oracle is executing. The simplest database in Oracle has one tablespace and one datafile.

The following are the three types of tablespaces in Oracle:

1. Permanent- this stores objects/segments that persist for more than the duration of the transaction or session. It is created using the CREATE TABLESPACE statement.

2. Undo- this stores objects/segments that are used in a transaction. They are very useful when one needs to rollback a particular transaction. It is created using the CREATE UNDO TABLESPACE statement.

3. Temporary- it stores objects/segments that only exist during a particular transaction or session. To create it, we

use the CREATE TEMPORARY TABLESPACE statement.

Each Oracle database must have two tablespaces:

1. SYSTEM- this tablespace stores metadata about segments (database dictionary). This helps the database to work correctly. This forms the first tablespace to be formed during database creation. The tablespace cannot be dropped and its name cannot be changed.

2. SYSAUX- this tablespace stores data for auxiliary Oracle applications and the operational data that is used for internal performance tools.

To create an Oracle tablespace, we use the CREATE TABLESPACE command which takes the following syntax:

CREATE TABLESPACE tablespace_name

[DATAFILE ´list of datafiles´ SIZE integer[K|M]]

[MINIMUM EXTENT integer[K|M]]

[BLOCKSIZE integer [K]]

[LOGGING|NOLOGGING]

[DEFAULT storage_clause]

[ONLINE|OFFLINE]

[PERMANENT|TEMPORARY/UNDO]

[EXTENT_MANAGEMENT_CLAUSE]

[SEGMENT_MANAGEMENT_CLAUSE]

[NEXT integer [K|M]]

[MAXSIZE integer [K|M]]

Note that in the above syntax, only the *tablespace_name* and DATAFILE clauses are mandatory. Let us discuss the uses of the various clauses in the above syntax:

1. DATAFILE and SIZE- specifies the list of datafiles together with their size.

2. MINIMUM EXTENT- each extent (contiguous data blocks) used will be a multiple of the specified number.

3. BLOCKSIZE- defines the blocksize of the tablespace.

4. LOGGING/NOLOGGING- the default one is logging, which means any changes to the segments will be written to redo logs.

5. DEFAULT- defines the default parameters for the segments that are created in the tablespace.

6. ONLINE/OFFLINE- the default is ONLINE, meaning the tablespace will be available for use.

7. PERMANENT/TEMPORARY/UNDO- this specifies the type of the tablespace, with PERMANENT being the default value.

8. EXTENT_MANAGEMENT_CLAUSE- this specifies how the extents will be managed.

9. SEGMENT_MANAGEMENT_CLAUSE- specifies how free and used space will be tracked in the segments.

10. NEXT- this specifies the size of next extent.

11. MAXSIZE- specifies the maximum disk space to be allocated to the tablespace. The default value is UNLIMITED.

Let us create a tablespace:

We should begin by created the file system structure in which we will store our data files. We will be using the *orcl* database to create a tablespace named *tbls01* in which we will store application data. The CREATE TABLESPACE statement should be as follows:

CREATE TABLESPACE tbls01 DATAFILE
'/app/centos/oradata/orcl/tbls01.dbf' SIZE 10M;

```
SQL> CREATE TABLESPACE tbls01 DATAFILE '/app/centos/oradata/orcl/tbls01.dbf' SIZE 10M;

Tablespace created.
```

If you navigate to the directory you have specified, you will find that the datafile for the tablespace has been created.

Note that we have not specified the extent size, the extent management and the segment space management options. Oracle 12c will choose the default options where segment space management will be done locally and automatically. To confirm this, run the following command:

SELECT extent_management, allocation_type,
segment_space_management FROM dba_tablespaces WHERE
tablespace_name= 'TBLS01';

```
SQL> SELECT extent_management, allocation_type, segment_space_management FROM db
a_tablespaces WHERE tablespace_name= 'TBLS01';

EXTENT_MAN ALLOCATIO SEGMEN
---------- --------- ------
LOCAL      SYSTEM    AUTO

SQL>
```

The size of a tablespace can be changed manually. For us to change the size of a data file associated to a tablespace manually, we use the RESIZE keyword and the ALTER DATABASE command. This is demonstrated below:

ALTER DATABASE DATAFILE
'/app/centos/oradata/orcl/tbls01.dbf' RESIZE 20M;

```
SQL> ALTER DATABASE DATAFILE '/app/centos/oradata/orcl/tbls01.dbf' RESIZE 20M;
Database altered.
```

When creating a tablespace, we can use the AUTOEXTEND provisioning mechanism to tell Oracle database to extend the data file size automatically to maximum or UNLIMITED size:

CREATE TABLESPACE tbls02 DATAFILE '/app/centos/oradata/orcl/tbls02.dbf' SIZE 10M

AUTOEXTEND ON

NEXT 10M

MAXSIZE 100M;

```
SQL> CREATE TABLESPACE tbls02 DATAFILE '/app/centos/oradata/orcl/tbls02.dbf' SIZE 10M
  2  AUTOEXTEND ON
  3  NEXT 10M
  4  MAXSIZE 100M;
Tablespace created.
```

BY default, each tablespace is readable and writable. To state that a tablespace cannot be written, we can make it read only. Example:

ALTER TABLESPACE tbls01 READ ONLY;

```
SQL> ALTER TABLESPACE tbls01 READ ONLY;
Tablespace altered.
SQL>
```

To make the tablespace writable, we should run the following command:

ALTER TABLESPACE tbls01 READ WRITE;

```
SQL> ALTER TABLESPACE tbls01 READ WRITE;
Tablespace altered.
SQL>
```

When a tablespace is taken offline, its data will be made unavailable to the users. This is very useful when you are performing backups, recoveries and moving datafiles without having to shut down the database. Example:

ALTER TABLESPACE tbls01 OFFLINE NORMAL;

The offline mode can be NORMAL, TEMPORARY, IMMEDIATE or FOR RECOVERY. To bring it online, we should run the following command:

ALTER TABLESPACE tbls01 ONLINE;

Redo Log and Archivelog

The log buffer is a circular buffer in SGA responsible for holding changes that are made to the database. The information is stored in redo entries. It determines the amount of memory in bytes that Oracle will use when buffering the redo entries to a redo log file. The redo log entries in Oracle stores all the changes made to the database in the order they occur. It is very useful for recovery options. Each instance in the Oracle database is associated with a redo log that protects the database in case an instance failure occurs.

The LGWR (Log Writer) process writes redo log entries from the log buffer to a redo log file. The redo logs are written in binary files, meaning you can't read them without the help of a software.

The redo logs are normally given a name ending with a .LOG or .RDO extension. They are also organized into groups and members. Each Oracle database should have at least two redo log groups. The redo log files have all the data necessary for you to recover lost data in your database. Every SQL statement that you run on your database changing data may be reconstructed by information saved in the redo log files.

When writing to the redo log files, the LGWR does it sequentially. It begins at the first fill and once filled up, it moves to write to the next file. The concept of *groups* comes from here. The LGWR fills one group and moves to the next one. Once all the groups are filled up, it moves to the first group.

When the redo log files are filled, Oracle allows you to save them in either online or offline destinations, and these are collectively referred to as "archived redo log". The process by which redo log files are turned into archived redo log files is known as "archiving". For the process to succeed, the database must be in ARCHIVELOG mode. Archived redo logs can be used for recovering a database, updating a standby database and for getting the history of a particular database by use of LogMiner utility.

A *log switch* occurs when one group is filled and the LGWR moves to write to another group. It can be forced by running the following command:

ALTER SYSTEM SWITCH LOGFILE;

The following are the views that provide us with information about redo log files:

1. V$LOG- shows the redo log file information from control file.

2. V$LOGFILE- identifies the redo log groups, members and the member status.

3. V$LOG_HISTORY- this stores information about the log history.

Run the following command:

SELECT * FROM V$LOG;

The query gives the control file information about the redo log for a database:

```
SQL> SELECT * FROM U$LOG;
    GROUP#   THREAD# SEQUENCE#      BYTES  BLOCKSIZE    MEMBERS ARC
STATUS            FIRST_CHANGE# FIRST_TIM NEXT_CHANGE# NEXT_TIME         CON_ID
         1         1         4  52428800        512          2 NO
INACTIVE          2358757 03-DEC-17     2373202 03-DEC-17                     0
         2         1         5  52428800        512          2 NO
INACTIVE          2373202 03-DEC-17     2383020 03-DEC-17                     0
         3         1         6  52428800        512          2 NO
CURRENT           2383020 03-DEC-17  2.8147E+14                              0

SQL>
```

To see information regarding redo log groups and members, run the following command:

SELECT * FROM V$LOGFILE;

If the field for STATUS is blank for a particular member, the file is in use.

To add a new group of redo log files, we use the ALTER DATABASE and ADD LOGFILE commands as shown below:

ALTER DATABASE ADD LOGFILE GROUP 5

('/app/centos/oradata/orcl/logfile1c.rdo',

'/app/centos/oradata/orcl/logfile2c.rdo')

SIZE 100M BLOCKSIZE 512;

```
SQL> ALTER DATABASE ADD LOGFILE GROUP 5
  2   ('/app/centos/oradata/orcl/logfile1c.rdo',
  3   '/app/centos/oradata/orcl/logfile2c.rdo')
  4   SIZE 100M BLOCKSIZE 512;

Database altered.
```

The redo log files will be identified by 5 as the group ID. To add a new member to a group, use the ALTER DATABASE and ADD LOGFILE MEMBER clauses as demonstrated below:

ALTER DATABASE ADD LOGFILE MEMBER

'/app/centos/oradata/orcl/logfile2b.rdo' TO GROUP 5;

```
SQL> ALTER DATABASE ADD LOGFILE MEMBER
  2  '/app/centos/oradata/orcl/logfile2b.rdo' TO GROUP 5;

Database altered.
```

The name of the file should be specified, but it's not a must for you to specify its size. Its file will be determined from the size of the other group members.

If you need to change the location of the redo log files, first shutdown the database. After the transfer, startup the database.

To rename a redo log file, use the ALTER DATABASE statement and combine it with RENAME FILE clause as demonstrated below:

First, start up the database, mount it but don't open it:

STARTUP MOUNT

Run the following command:

ALTER DATABASE RENAME FILE
/app/centos/oradata/orcl/logfile1c.rdo',
/app/centos/oradata/orcl/logfile2c.rdo' TO '
/app/centos/oradata/orcl/logfile1d.rdo', '
/app/centos/oradata/orcl/logfile2d.rdo';

The two redo log files will be renamed. You can then open your database for the changes to take effect:

ALTER DATABASE OPEN;

To delete a particular group of redo log files, run the following command:

ALTER DATABASE DROP LOGFILE GROUP 5;

All the redo log files belonging to group 5 will be dropped.

```
SQL> ALTER DATABASE DROP LOGFILE GROUP 5;

Database altered.

SQL>
```

To change the database state to ARCHIVELOG mode, first shut it down:

SHUTDOWN IMMEDIATE

Start a new instance, mount, but don't open the database;

STARTUP MOUNT

Change the state of the database to archiving mode then open it for normal operations:

ALTER DATABASE ARCHIVELOG;

ALTER DATABASE OPEN;

```
SQL> SHUTDOWN IMMEDIATE
Database closed.
Database dismounted.
ORACLE instance shut down.
SQL> STARTUP MOUNT
ORACLE instance started.

Total System Global Area   843055104 bytes
Fixed Size                   3051232 bytes
Variable Size              566231328 bytes
Database Buffers           268435456 bytes
Redo Buffers                 5337088 bytes
Database mounted.
SQL> ALTER DATABASE ARCHIVELOG;

Database altered.

SQL> ALTER DATABASE OPEN;

Database altered.

SQL>
```

To do a manual archiving, replace the above ALTER DATABASE command with the following command:

ALTER DATABASE ARCHIVELOG MANUAL;

Next, connect to the database with sydba privileges, then run the following command to archive all the filled redo log files:

ALTER SYSTEM ARCHIVE LOG ALL;

Note that you should mount or open the database.

Undo Tablespace

Each Oracle database should have a way of maintaining the information that is used to undo or roll back the changes to the database. The information has records of the actions of transactions before they can be committed. The records are referred to as undo.

If you had not created an undo tablespace when creating the database, run the following command to create one:

SQL> create undo tablespace untbs01 datafile

'/app/centos/oradata/orcl/undo_tbs.dbf'

size 500M autoextend ON next 5M;

```
SQL> create undo tablespace untbs01 datafile
  2   '/app/centos/oradata/orcl/undo_tbs.dbf'
  3   size 500M autoextend ON next 5M;

Tablespace created.
```

Shut down the database, then add the following to your parameter file:

UNDO_MANAGEMENT=AUTO
UNDO_TABLESPACE=untbs01

Save and start the Oracle database.

To drop the undo tablespace, run the following command:

DROP TABLESPACE untbs01;

It is also possible for you to switch from using a particular undo tablespace to another. The following command demonstrates how this can be done:

ALTER SYSTEM SET UNDO_TABLESPACE = untbs01;

```
SQL> ALTER SYSTEM SET UNDO_TABLESPACE = untbs01;
System altered.
SQL>
```

The instance will then begin to use untbs01 as the current undo tablespace.

The following query can help you see the number of active transactions in the undo tablespace:

SQL> select * from v$transaction;

Statistics regarding tuning of the undo tablespace can be viewed by running the following command:

SQL> select * from v$undostat;

```
SQL> select * from v$undostat;

BEGIN_TIM END_TIME    UNDOTON    UNDOBLKS    TXNCOUNT MAXQUERYLEN MAXQUERYID
MAXCONCURRENCY UNXPSTEALCNT UNXPBLKRELCNT UNXPBLKREUCNT EXPSTEALCNT EXPBLKRELCNT

EXPBLKREUCNT SSOLDERRCNT NOSPACEERRCNT ACTIVEBLKS UNEXPIREDBLKS EXPIREDBLKS
TUNED_UNDORETENTION    CON_ID
03-DEC-17 03-DEC-17         7         43        311         321 0rc4km05kgzb9
           3               0          0                    0                 0
           0               0          0        288                    0        0
                981                   0

SQL>
```

Chapter 5- Oracle Database Operations

Startup Database

To startup an Oracle database, we use the "startup" command. You must be logged into an account with sysdba or sysoper privileges like the SYS account. The following example shows a DBA connecting to the database and starting up an instance on SQL Plus:

```
SQL Plus

SQL*Plus: Release 12.1.0.2.0 Production on Sat Dec 16 16:36:15 2017

Copyright (c) 1982, 2014, Oracle.  All rights reserved.

Enter user-name: sys as sysdba
Enter password:
Connected to an idle instance.

SQL> startup
ORACLE instance started.

Total System Global Area    843055104 bytes
Fixed Size                    3051232 bytes
Variable Size               566231328 bytes
Database Buffers            268435456 bytes
Redo Buffers                  5337088 bytes
Database mounted.
Database opened.
SQL>
```

To connect and startup the database from the command prompt (In my case I am using Windows), you must first set the oracle_sid to the name of the database you need to connect to. Next, you should connect to the database with sysdba or sysoper privileges then startup the database as follows:

```
C:\Windows\system32\cmd.exe - sqlplus "sys as sysdba"                    _  □  ☒

Microsoft Windows [Version 6.1.7601]
Copyright (c) 2009 Microsoft Corporation.  All rights reserved.

C:\Users\admin>set oracle_sid=orcl

C:\Users\admin>sqlplus "sys as sysdba"

SQL*Plus: Release 12.1.0.2.0 Production on Sat Dec 16 16:42:51 2017

Copyright (c) 1982, 2014, Oracle.  All rights reserved.

Enter password:
Connected to an idle instance.

SQL> startup
ORACLE instance started.

Total System Global Area   843055104 bytes
Fixed Size                   3051232 bytes
Variable Size              566231328 bytes
Database Buffers           268435456 bytes
Redo Buffers                 5337088 bytes
Database mounted.
Database opened.
SQL>
```

Stop DB

You should shut down the oracle database before shutting down the system and before carrying out full backups. To stop the database, we use the "shutdown" command. The following are the types of shutdowns in Oracle:

- SHUTDOWN NORMAL (or just SHUTDOWN)- the database will prohibit new connects, wait for all users to disconnect, then close and dismount the database, then closes the database instance.

- SHUTDOWN IMMEDIATE- this cancels the current calls like system interrupt, closes and dismounts the database. Finally, it closes the database instance.

- SHUTDOWN ABORT- this waits for nothing, but its shuts down the database now. On startup, the DBA should recover the instance.

To use any of the above shutdown methods, you just issue the "shutdown" command followed by the type of shutdown you need. The following example shows how a "SHUTDOWN

IMMEDIATE" can be used:

```
SQL> shutdown immediate
Database closed.
Database dismounted.
ORACLE instance shut down.
SQL>
```

Update Configuration Parameters

To see all the configuration parameters of your oracle database, run the following command:

SQL> SHOW PARAMETERS

Each parameter will have a name, type and value. If you need to see all the parameters with "block" in their names, run the following command:

SQL> SHOW PARAMETERS BLOCK

You can open the initialization parameter file in a text editor and edit its parameters. The changes will take effect after the database is restarted. To update a server parameter file, use the following command:

SQL> ALTER SYSTEM SET ... SCOPE=SPFILE

If you need to remove a parameter from server parameter file, use the following command:

SQL> ALTER SYSTEM RESET ... SCOPE=SPFILE

In the above case, the default value for the parameter will be used the next time you start the database.

It is possible for you to modify some parameters using ALTER SESSION or ALTER SYSTEM statements while the instance is up and running. You can use the following syntax to modify initialization parameters:

SQL> ALTER SESSION SET parameter_name = value

SQL> ALTER SYSTEM SET parameter_name = value [DEFERRED]

The ALTER SESSION command will change the value of a parameter for the duration of session that invokes the statement.

Grant/Revoke Access

Grant is used to grant privileges on objects such as tables, procedures, views and others to other users or roles.

Suppose you are the owner of a table named "COUNTRIES". You need to grant grant select, update and insert privileges to a user named "OE" on this table. Use the following command:

SQL> grant select, update, insert on COUNTRIES to OE;

```
SQL> grant select, update, insert on COUNTRIES to OE;

Grant succeeded.
```

If you need to grant all privileges on the table "COUNTRIES" to user "OE", use the following command:

SQL> grant all on COUNTRIES to OE;

```
SQL> grant all on COUNTRIES to OE;

Grant succeeded.
```

If you need all database users to be able to view the contents of the "COUNTRIES" table, you can grant all of them a "select" privilege by running the following command:

SQL> grant select on COUNTRIES to public;

```
SQL> grant select on COUNTRIES to public;

Grant succeeded.
```

It is also possible for you to grant different permissions on different columns of the same table.

Suppose you need to grant insert permission on the region_id column of table "COUNTRIES" and update permission on country_name column of the same table to user "OE", run the following command:

SQL> grant update (country_name),insert (region_id) on COUNTRIES to OE;

```
SQL> grant update (country_name),insert (region_id)  on COUNTRIES to OE;

Grant succeeded.
```

Suppose you need to grant the select privilege to the user OE on table "COUNTRIES" and make OE be able to pass on the privilege to the other users, you should run the command with "GRANT OPTION" as shown below:

SQL> grant select on COUNTRIES to OE with grant option;

```
SQL> grant select on COUNTRIES to OE with grant option;

Grant succeeded.
```

The "REVOKE" command is used to revoke the privileges that have been assigned to users.

Example, to revote the select, update and insert privileges that you have granted to OE on table Student, run the following command:

SQL> revoke select, update, insert on COUNTRIES from OE;

```
SQL> revoke select, update, insert on COUNTRIES from OE;

Revoke succeeded.
```

To revoke the select privilege we granted to the public on table Student, run the following command:

SQL> revoke select on COUNTRIES from public;

```
SQL> revoke select on student from public;
Revoke succeeded.
SQL>
```

To revoke the insert permission on the name column of table "Student" and update permission on name and age columns, run the following command:

SQL> revoke update, insert on COUNTRIES from OE;

```
SQL> revoke update, insert on COUNTRIES from OE;

Revoke succeeded.
```

Note that if you try to revoke a privilege that is not available, you will get an error. In the last command given above, be keen as you might have revoked the update and insert privileges from OE on table COUNTRIES.

Monitor Audit Trails

In oracle, auditing is one of the security measures, and it involves recording of database activity. It allows the DBA to track the activity of a user in the database. The records are written in a table named AUD$ and it is owned by SYS. The SYS.AUD$ (dba_audit_trail) and the dba_fga_audit_trail are popularly known as the *audit trail.*

All users can be audited except SYS and CONNECT INTERNAL users. Auditing can only be done on users who are connected directly to the database but not for actions on a remote database.

To enable or disable auditing, we use the AUDIT_TRAIL database initialization parameter. It has a default setting of NONE, meaning that auditing is not done. To enable auditing, the value of this parameter should be set to DB or OS. If it is set to DB, then records will be send to the SYS.AUD$ table, while if set to OS, the records will be send ti an operating system file. However, not all operating systems support the OS option.

The "audit" command normally writes the auditing information to certain data dictionary views. Check the following tables where such information is entered:

1. dba_audit_exists

2. dba_audit_object

3. dba_audit_session

4. dba_audit_statement

5. dba_audit_trail

In the previous versions of Oracle, the audit trails for the various components were kept separately. Examples of such audit trails include:

- SYS.AUD$- this is for the database audit trail,

- SYS.FGA_LOG$- used in fine-grained auditing

- DVSYS.AUDIT_TRAIL$ - used for Oracle Database Vault, Oracle Label Security, etc.

In Oracle 12c, the audit trails have been combined into one, which can be viewed from UNIFIED_AUDIT_TRAIL data dictionary view for both single-instance installations and Oracle Database Real Application Clusters environments. This provides the Oracle DBAs with an effective way to audit the audit logs.

To audit all DML (inserts, updates, deletes), DDL (create table) and login/logoff events by the user HR, we can run the following command:

SQL> audit all by HR by access;

```
SQL> audit all by HR by access;

Audit succeeded.
```

To Audit all the viewing activity by the user HR, use the following command:

SQL> audit select table by HR by access;

```
SQL> audit select table by HR by access;

Audit succeeded.
```

To audit any activity by user HR that changes table data, we run the following command:

audit update table, delete table,
insert table by HR by access;

```
SQL> audit update table, delete table,
  2          insert table by HR by access;

Audit succeeded.
```

To see the auditing information that has been recorded, you only have to query for the contents of dba_audit-trail table. First, you can describe the table to know its columns:

SQL> desc dba_audit_trail

```
SQL> desc dba_audit_trail;
 Name                           Null?    Type
                                         
 OS_USERNAME                             VARCHAR2(255)
 USERNAME                                VARCHAR2(128)
 USERHOST                                VARCHAR2(128)
 TERMINAL                                VARCHAR2(255)
 TIMESTAMP                               DATE
 OWNER                                   VARCHAR2(128)
 OBJ_NAME                                VARCHAR2(128)
 ACTION                         NOT NULL NUMBER
 ACTION_NAME                             VARCHAR2(28)
 NEW_OWNER                               VARCHAR2(128)
 NEW_NAME                                VARCHAR2(128)
 OBJ_PRIVILEGE                           VARCHAR2(16)
 SYS_PRIVILEGE                           VARCHAR2(40)
 ADMIN_OPTION                            VARCHAR2(1)
```

The table has numerous columns, so you don't have to view all. The following command shows how to view a number of columns of the table:

SQL> select username, action_name, timestamp from dba_audit_trail;

Chapter 6- Oracle Database Built-in Software

SqlPlus

This is an interactive and batch query tool that comes with every installation Oracle database. It is made up of a command-line user interface, a Windows Graphical User Interface (GUI) and iSQL*Plus web-based user interface.

SqlPlus helps us access the Oracle database. You can enter then execute SQL, PL/SQL, SQL*Plus as well as operating system commands on SqlPlus.

To start SqlPlus, click Start > All Programs, then identify the installation of your oracle database. Click it. In my case, this is named "Oracle- OraDB12Home1. Click it, then "Application Development". Click "SQL Plus". You be asked to login using your username and password.

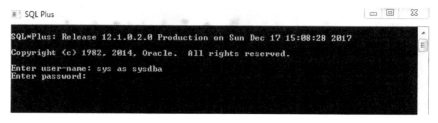

After a successful login, the SQL terminal will be presented to you. Note that the password will not be shown in the form of asterisk characters (*) as you type it, that is, it is silent. This is for security purposes:

You can then run your commands on the terminal.

RMAN

For your database to stay protected, you must create its backup and know how to recover it. This can be done using Oracle RMAN (Recovery Manager) tool.

Starting RMAN

To start RMAN, open the command prompt of your operating system then run the following command:

rman target=/

You will be presented with the RMAN prompt:

To see the default configuration of RMAN, run the following command:

RMAN> show all;

TKPROF

TKPROF is an acronym for Transient Kernel PROFile and it is used to format a trace file into a readable format. It is normally set via *sql_trace* parameter. To get the most out of this utility, you should enable time statistics by running the following command:

SQL> ALTER SYSTEM SET TIMED_STATISTICS = TRUE;

```
SQL> ALTER SYSTEM SET TIMED_STATISTICS = TRUE;
System altered.
SQL>
```

The above will enable the collection of vital statistics like CPU execution time, wait events, and elapsed times.

Oracle can generate many and large trace files, which are normally kept under the *user_dump_dest* directory as defined in the init.ora file. The default setting is that tracing is disabled due to the burden that it adds to the database. To enable tracing, run the following command:

SQL> ALTER SESSION SET SQL_TRACE = TRUE;

```
SQL>  ALTER SESSION SET SQL_TRACE = TRUE;
Session altered.
```

After tracing with Oracle TKPROF has been enabled, Oracle will generate and store the statistics in the trace file.

To disable tracing, run the following command:

ALTER SESSION SET SQL_TRACE = FALSE;

```
SQL>  ALTER SESSION SET SQL_TRACE = FALSE;
Session altered.
SQL>
```

Chapter 7- Oracle Database Backup and Restore

Export/Import using EXPDP/IMPDP

The Oracle Data Pump (expdp and impdp) is used for exporting and importing Oracle databases. With the expdp utility, we can export data or unload data or its metadata from one database to another.

To perform a database export with expdp, begin by creating a folder. It is recommended that you don't create the folder in the Oracle home directory or in the directory with the OS bootable files. In my case, I have created the folder at "F:\Export".

Next, we should create the directory object and grant the necessary privileges. Login to the database with sysdba privileges. We can run the CREATE DIRECTORY command in order to create the directory object:

SQL> CREATE DIRECTORY orcl_full AS '/dpdump';

```
SQL> CREATE DIRECTORY orcl_full AS '/dpdump';

Directory created.
```

The orcl_full is just a name that will be mapped to the directory path, so you can use any name that you want.

Next, we should grant read and write permissions on the directory to the user we need to perform the export. In our case, this is HR:

SQL> GRANT read, write ON DIRECTORY orcl_full TO HR;

```
SQL> GRANT read, write ON DIRECTORY orcl_full TO HR;

Grant succeeded.
```

For HR to be able to perform a full export of the database, he must have the DATAPUMP_EXP_FULL_DATABASE role. We can then grant him this role:

SQL> GRANT DATAPUMP_EXP_FULL_DATABASE TO HR;

```
SQL> GRANT DATAPUMP_EXP_FULL_DATABASE TO HR;

Grant succeeded.
```

We are then done with all the settings, so we can export the database. Type the "exit" command on the SQL terminal to go back to the operating system prompt then run the following command:

**C:\>expdp HR@ORCL2 DIRECTORY=orcl_full
DUMPFILE=orclfull.dmp LOGFILE=full_exp.log;**

```
C:\Users\Billy>expdp HR@ORCL2 DIRECTORY=orcl_full DUMPFILE=orclfull.dmp LOGFILE=full_exp.log;

Export: Release 12.2.0.1.0 - Production on Sun Dec 31 11:23:13 2017

Copyright (c) 1982, 2017, Oracle and/or its affiliates.  All rights reserved.
Password:
```

Type the password for the user then hit enter key. The backup will be done.

At **HR@ORCL2,** HR is the name of the user exporting the database, while ORCL is the SID (Site Identifier) of the database to be imported. The DIRECTORY parameter helps us specify the directory to which we need to export the database. We have also specified the named to be used for the dump file and the log file.

The impdp utility helps in loading an export dump file set to a target system. It is invoked by running the impdb command. Consider the following command:

SQL> impdp HR@orcl2 directory=orcl_full
DUMPFILE=orclfull.dmp LOGFILE=full_exp.log;

The above command can be used to import the database that we exported with the expdp command. The dump file and the log file must be the same to what was used in the expdp command in order to help the utility locate the files of the database.

RMAN

The RMAN tool can be used for backup and recovery of databases in Oracle. If the database is running in ARCHIVELOG mode, then we can backup the database while it is open. This is known as an "inconsistent backup" and a redo will be required during the recovery process in order to bring the database to a consistent state.

The following command will back up the oracle database together with all the archived redo log file to the default backup device:

RMAN> BACKUP DATABASE PLUS ARCHIVELOG;

```
RMAN> BACKUP DATABASE PLUS ARCHIVELOG;

Starting backup at 30-DEC-17
current log archived
using target database control file instead of recovery catalog
allocated channel: ORA_DISK_1
channel ORA_DISK_1: SID=256 device type=DISK
channel ORA_DISK_1: starting archived log backup set
channel ORA_DISK_1: specifying archived log(s) in backup set
input archived log thread=1 sequence=122 RECID=17 STAMP=961434869
input archived log thread=1 sequence=123 RECID=18 STAMP=961452026
input archived log thread=1 sequence=124 RECID=19 STAMP=961549253
input archived log thread=1 sequence=125 RECID=20 STAMP=961582507
input archived log thread=1 sequence=126 RECID=21 STAMP=961617645
```

centos@centos7:~

The output from the command will also the location of the backup files. When I navigate to the directory at operating system level, I find the files as follows:

```
                     centos@centos7:/app/centos/recovery_area/ORCL/
 File   Edit   View   Search   Terminal   Help
[centos@centos7 ~]$ cd /app/centos/recovery_area/ORCL/backupset/
[centos@centos7 backupset]$ ls
2017_11_30   2017_12_30
[centos@centos7 backupset]$ cd 2017_12_30/
[centos@centos7 2017_12_30]$ ls
o1_mf_annnn_TAG20171230T192942_f4jpf6z2_.bkp
o1_mf_annnn_TAG20171230T193142_f4jpjyks_.bkp
o1_mf_ncsnf_TAG20171230T192944_f4jpjx83_.bkp
o1_mf_nnndf_TAG20171230T192944_f4jpf89l_.bkp
[centos@centos7 2017_12_30]$ █
```

If the database runs in the NOARCHIVELOG mode, then we have to perform a "consistent" backup. To do this, we should first mount the database after a consistent shutdown. There will be no need for recovery once the database is restored.

Let us demonstrate how this can be done:

Begin by shutting down your database consistently then mount it. We need to ensure that the database is in a consistent state for a backup:

RMAN> SHUTDOWN IMMEDIATE;

RMAN> STARTUP FORCE DBA;

RMAN> SHUTDOWN IMMEDIATE;

RMAN> STARTUP MOUNT;

```
RMAN> shutdown immediate;

database closed
database dismounted
Oracle instance shut down

RMAN> STARTUP FORCE DBA;

Oracle instance started
database mounted
database opened

Total System Global Area      843055104 bytes

Fixed Size                      3051232 bytes
Variable Size                 570425632 bytes
Database Buffers              264241152 bytes
Redo Buffers                    5337088 bytes

RMAN> SHUTDOWN IMMEDIATE;

database closed
database dismounted
Oracle instance shut down

RMAN> STARTUP MOUNT;

connected to target database (not started)
Oracle instance started
database mounted

Total System Global Area      843055104 bytes

Fixed Size                      3051232 bytes
Variable Size                 566231328 bytes
Database Buffers              268435456 bytes
Redo Buffers                    5337088 bytes

RMAN>
```

Next, execute the "DATABASE BACKUP" command. The backup will be created in the default location:

RMAN> BACKUP DATABASE;

```
RMAN> BACKUP DATABASE;

Starting backup at 30-DEC-17
using channel ORA_DISK_1
channel ORA_DISK_1: starting full datafile backup set
channel ORA_DISK_1: specifying datafile(s) in backup set
input datafile file number=00005 name=/app/centos/oradata/orcl/example01.dbf
input datafile file number=00003 name=/app/centos/oradata/orcl/sysaux01.dbf
input datafile file number=00001 name=/app/centos/oradata/orcl/system01.dbf
input datafile file number=00008 name=/app/centos/oradata/orcl/undo_tbs.dbf
input datafile file number=00004 name=/app/centos/oradata/orcl/undotbs01.dbf
input datafile file number=00002 name=/app/centos/oradata/orcl/tbls01.dbf
input datafile file number=00007 name=/app/centos/oradata/orcl/tbls02.dbf
input datafile file number=00006 name=/app/centos/oradata/orcl/users01.dbf
channel ORA_DISK_1: starting piece 1 at 30-DEC-17
```

| centos@centos7:~ | centos@centos7:/app/centos/recov... |

You can then run the following command to open the database and resume the normal operation:

RMAN> ALTER DATABASE OPEN;

```
RMAN> ALTER DATABASE OPEN;

Statement processed

RMAN>
```

Whenever you need to delete obsolete backups, which is another way of saying that that the tape management system has expired the file. Therefore, the backup piece is expired as well and no longer required even though the file still exists. You just open RMAN then run the following command:

RMAN> DELETE OBSOLETE;

```
RMAN> delete obsolete;

RMAN retention policy will be applied to the command
RMAN retention policy is set to recovery window of 1 days
using channel ORA_DISK_1
no obsolete backups found
```

You can configure RMAN to back up the SPFILE and the control file automatically by running the following command:

RMAN>configure controlfile autobackup on;

To recover and restore databases, we use the RESTORE and RECOVER commands. Restoring data files refers to retrieving them from backups as they are needed for a recovery operation. Recovery involves the application of changes from redo logs to a restored data file in order to bring forward the data file to a desired point in time.

Restore and recovery with RMAN can be done as follows:

Start RMAN then connect to the target database.

If you wish, run the following command to show the current tablespaces and data files:

RMAN> REPORT SCHEMA;

```
RMAN> report schema;

using target database control file instead of recovery catalog
Report of database schema for database with db_unique_name ORCL

List of Permanent Datafiles
===========================
File Size(MB) Tablespace          RB segs Datafile Name
---- -------- ------------------- ------- ------------------------
1    810      SYSTEM              YES     /app/centos/oradata/orcl/system01.dbf
2    20       TBLS01              NO      /app/centos/oradata/orcl/tbls01.dbf
3    1070     SYSAUX              NO      /app/centos/oradata/orcl/sysaux01.dbf
4    180      UNDOTBS1            YES     /app/centos/oradata/orcl/undotbs01.dbf
5    1243     EXAMPLE             NO      /app/centos/oradata/orcl/example01.dbf
6    5        USERS               NO      /app/centos/oradata/orcl/users01.dbf
7    10       TBLS02              NO      /app/centos/oradata/orcl/tbls02.dbf
8    500      UNTBS01             YES     /app/centos/oradata/orcl/undo_tbs.dbf

List of Temporary Files
=======================
File Size(MB) Tablespace          Maxsize(MB) Tempfile Name
---- -------- ------------------- ----------- ------------------------
1    197      TEMP                32767       /app/centos/oradata/orcl/temp01.dbf
```

Run the RESTORE DATABASE command and add the PREVIEW option to it. We will also add the SUMMARY option so that the metadata is not displayed verbosely:

RMAN> RESTORE DATABASE PREVIEW SUMMARY;

```
RMAN> RESTORE DATABASE PREVIEW SUMMARY;

Starting restore at 17-DEC-17
using channel ORA_DISK_1

List of Backups
===============
Key     TY LV S Device Type Completion Time #Pieces #Copies Compressed Tag
---     -- -- - ----------- --------------- ------- ------- ---------- ---
5        B  F  A DISK        17-DEC-17       1       1       NO         TAG201712
17T163650
archived logs generated after SCN 2881947 not found in repository
RMAN-05119: recovery can not be done to a consistent state.
Media recovery start SCN is 2881947
Recovery must be done beyond SCN 2881947 to clear datafile fuzziness
Finished restore at 17-DEC-17

RMAN>
```

If you need to restore the whole database, then you must put the database in mount state. You should run the following sequence of commands:

RMAN> STARTUP FORCE MOUNT;

RMAN> RESTORE DATABASE;

RMAN> RECOVER DATABASE;

RMAN> ALTER DATABASE OPEN;

ASM

ASM (Automatic Storage Management) is a file system and volume manager for Oracle database capable of supporting Oracle Real Application Clusters (Oracle RAC) and a single-instance Oracle database. It is the recommended solution for storage management in Oracle.

In ASM, the storage of datafiles is done in "disk groups". A disk group in ASM is simply a collection of disks that ASM manages as a unit. The contents of files stored in a disk group are distributed evenly or striped in order to eliminate hot spots and provide a uniform performance across the disks. This gives it a better performance compared to when using raw devices.

Mirroring is a way of protecting the integrity of data by storing copies of the data on multiple disks. When creating an ASK disk group, you must state the Oracle ASM disk group type depending on these three levels of redundancy:

- Normal- this is for 2-way mirroring

- High- this is for 3-way mirroring

- External- to avoid using Oracle ASM mirroring, like when you configure hardware RAID for redundancy.

Failure groups are used to store mirrored copies of data in such a way that every copy is on a disk in a different failure group. A simultaneous failure of all disks in a particular failure group will not lead into a data loss.

To create a disk group, we use the CREATE DISKGROUP statement. The statement will allow you to specify the level of redundancy. The following command can be used to create a disk group:

CREATE DISKGROUP data NORMAL REDUNDANCY

FAILGROUP controller1 DISK

'/devices/diska1' NAME diska1;

Recovery Catalogue

A recovery catalogue is simply a database schema that is used by RMAN to store the metadata about the other Oracle databases. It tracks backups and stores scripts that will be used by RMAN in backup and recovery situations.

The RMAN schema owner should be created in the RMAN database by following the steps given below:

Login to the database with administrator privileges:

```
C:\Users\admin>sqlplus sys as sysdba
SQL*Plus: Release 12.1.0.2.0 Production on Mon Dec 18 17:42:15 2017
Copyright (c) 1982, 2014, Oracle. All rights reserved.
Enter password:
```

Next, create a user and a schema for the recovery catalog as shown below:

CREATE USER rman IDENTIFIED BY Password
TEMPORARY TABLESPACE temp
DEFAULT TABLESPACE tools
QUOTA UNLIMITED ON tools;

```
SQL> CREATE USER rman IDENTIFIED BY Password
  2      TEMPORARY TABLESPACE temp
  3      DEFAULT TABLESPACE tools
  4      QUOTA UNLIMITED ON tools;
```

Grant the role "recovery_catalog_owner" to the user. The role will give the user all the privileges that are necessary for him to maintain the recovery catalog.

SQL> GRANT RECOVERY_CATALOG_OWNER TO rman;

```
SQL> GRANT RECOVERY_CATALOG_OWNER TO rman;
Grant succeeded.
SQL>
```

Now that we have created the user, we can add the recovery catalog schema.

Start the RMAN then connect as the "rman" user we have created above:

rman target /

```
C:\Users\admin>rman target /
Recovery Manager: Release 12.1.0.2.0 - Production on Mon Dec 18 17:53:57 2017
Copyright (c) 1982, 2014, Oracle and/or its affiliates.  All rights reserved.
connected to target database: ORCL (DBID=1489472328)
```

RMAN> CONNECT CATALOG rman@orcl

Type the password you created for user "rman".

RMAN> CREATE CATALOG;

Use the same RMAN session to connect the RMAN using operating system authentication then register the database in the database by running the REGISTER CATALOG command:

RMAN> CONNECT TARGET /

RMAN> REGISTER DATABASE;

RMAN> EXIT

Chapter 8- Oracle Database Tuning

Soft vs Hard Parse

If an SQL statement that does not exist in the shared pool is executed during a session, then Oracle has to do a "hard parse". Oracle must assign some memory space to the statement from the pool, check the syntax of the statement and check whether the user trying to execute the statement has the necessary permissions to do so. A hard parse is expensive in terms of CPU used.

If an SQL statement that exists in the shared pool is executed during a session, this means that there is a version of the statement that can be used, and this is known as a "soft parse".

For a soft parse to occur, the two SQL statements must be exactly identical even in terms of case. Consider the following SQL statements:

select x from y;

SELECT X FROM Y;

The two statements are not identical because one is written in uppercase while the other is written in lowercase. If the two statements are executed, then a hard parse will occur.

TKPROF

Tkprof does not control the contents of the trace file, but it simply formats them. There are multiple ways in Oracle to generate the trace file. Tkprof is very valuable for a detailed trace file analysis. You do a detailed dump using the TKPROF utility and setting the parameter *sql_trace=true*.

The trace files generated by Oracle are placed in the User Dump Destination directory.

You can also use the ALTER SESSION command to specify this directory for a particular session. To check the location of the directory, run the following command:

SQL> show parameter USER_DUMP_DEST;

```
SQL> show parameter USER_DUMP_DEST;

NAME                                 TYPE        VALUE
------------------------------------ ----------- ------------------------------
user_dump_dest                       string      /app/centos/product/12.1.0/dbh
                                                 ome_1/rdbms/log
```

ASH

The Active Session History (ASH) was introduced in Oracle 10g. It was developed for use in diagnostics and tuning the Oracle database. The ASH gets information from [G]V$ to enable you see the current and historical information about the active sessions on the database.

The active session history is snapped once every second in gv_$active_session_history table. It is held for about 30 minutes then stored in dba_hist_active_sess_history table. Samples of the wait event information are made available via the V$ACTIVE_SESSION_HISTORY view. It is a fact table that can be linked to various dimensions in order to provide statistics regarding a number of things including execution plans, SQL statements, wait events, objects, modules, sessions, actions, services, client identifiers, consumer groups etc.

It can help you know what the active sessions are doing, or what they have done. Example, if I need to know the main activity of the database in the last 5 minutes, I can run the following command:

SELECT NVL(a.event, 'ON CPU') AS event,

COUNT(*) AS total_wait_time

FROM v$active_session_history a

WHERE a.sample_time > SYSDATE - 5/(24*60) -- 5 mins

GROUP BY a.event

ORDER BY total_wait_time DESC;

```
SQL> SELECT NUL(a.event, 'ON CPU') AS event,
  2         COUNT(*) AS total_wait_time
  3    FROM v$active_session_history a
  4   WHERE a.sample_time > SYSDATE - 5/(24*60) -- 5 mins
  5   GROUP BY a.event
  6   ORDER BY total_wait_time DESC;

EVENT                                                           TOTAL_WAIT_TIME
--------------------------------------------------------------  ---------------
ON CPU                                                                        2
log file parallel write                                                      1
oracle thread bootstrap                                                      1
control file parallel write                                                  1
db file parallel write                                                       1

SQL>
```

You notice that the total wait times are accumulating with every sample. If you sum them all, you will get a false high value. The time columns in the ASH views are a bit complicated so they should be interpreted more keenly.

To provide a historical access to the ASH data, one in every 10 samples is persisted in the disk and made available via the DBA_HIST_ACTIVE_SESS_HISTORY view. This makes it a sample of a sample. To see the various columns of the view, describe it. This is demonstrated below:

```
SQL> desc dba_hist_active_sess_history
 Name                               Null?      Type
 SNAP_ID                            NOT NULL   NUMBER
 DBID                               NOT NULL   NUMBER
 INSTANCE_NUMBER                    NOT NULL   NUMBER
 SAMPLE_ID                          NOT NULL   NUMBER
 SAMPLE_TIME                        NOT NULL   TIMESTAMP(3)
 SESSION_ID                         NOT NULL   NUMBER
 SESSION_SERIAL#                               NUMBER
 SESSION_TYPE                                  VARCHAR2(10)
 FLAGS                                         NUMBER
 USER_ID                                       NUMBER
 SQL_ID                                        VARCHAR2(13)
 IS_SQLID_CURRENT                              VARCHAR2(1)
 SQL_CHILD_NUMBER                              NUMBER
 SQL_OPCODE                                    NUMBER
 SQL_OPNAME                                    VARCHAR2(64)
 FORCE_MATCHING_SIGNATURE                      NUMBER
 TOP_LEVEL_SQL_ID                              VARCHAR2(13)
 TOP_LEVEL_SQL_OPCODE                          NUMBER
 SQL_PLAN_HASH_VALUE                           NUMBER
 SQL_FULL_PLAN_HASH_VALUE                      NUMBER
 SQL_ADAPTIVE_PLAN_RESOLVED                    NUMBER
 SQL_PLAN_LINE_ID                              NUMBER
 SQL_PLAN_OPERATION                            VARCHAR2(64)
 SQL_PLAN_OPTIONS                              VARCHAR2(64)
 SQL_EXEC_ID                                   NUMBER
 SQL_EXEC_START                                DATE
 PLSQL_ENTRY_OBJECT_ID                         NUMBER
 PLSQL_ENTRY_SUBPROGRAM_ID                     NUMBER
 PLSQL_OBJECT_ID                               NUMBER
 PLSQL_SUBPROGRAM_ID                           NUMBER
 QC_INSTANCE_ID                                NUMBER
 QC_SESSION_ID                                 NUMBER
```

This view is similar to the V$ACTIVE_SESSION_HISTORY view, but the sample time in this case is 10 seconds. This means you should use (count*10) when measuring time instead of just count as shown below:

SELECT NVL(a.event, 'ON CPU') AS event,

COUNT(*)*10 AS total_wait_time

FROM dba_hist_active_sess_history a

WHERE a.sample_time > SYSDATE - 1

GROUP BY a.event

ORDER BY total_wait_time DESC;

```
SQL> SELECT NUL(a.event, 'ON CPU') AS event,
   2         COUNT(*)*10 AS total_wait_time
   3  FROM   dba_hist_active_sess_history a
   4  WHERE  a.sample_time > SYSDATE - 1
   5  GROUP BY a.event
   6  ORDER BY total_wait_time DESC;

EVENT                                          TOTAL_WAIT_TIME
---------------------------------------------- ---------------

ON CPU                                                    1000

control file sequential read                              500

db file sequential read                                   410

enq: PV - syncstart                                       280

oracle thread bootstrap                                   220

enq: PR - contention                                      150

read by other session                                      80

control file parallel write                                70

external table read                                        40

latch: row cache objects                                   40

log file parallel write                                    40

EVENT                                          TOTAL_WAIT_TIME
---------------------------------------------- ---------------

buffer busy waits                                          30
```

It is of great importance for you to directly access the ASH information. There are various ways through which you can get this information. A good example is OEM (Oracle Enterprise Manager) which provides you with an easy access to real-time and historical performance information.

The OEM is normally accessed from the client browser, and the dbconsole process should be running. If the dbconsole process is not started on your Linux system, navigate as follows to start it:

1. Navigate into ORACLE_HOME/bin directory.

2. Run the following statement:

./emctl start dbconsole

To view the status of this process, run the following command on the Linux OS terminal:

./emctl status dbconsole

To stop it, run the following command:

./emctl stop dbconsole

On Windows, the service can be started and stopped from the Windows service dialog which you can access by navigating as follows:

1. Click **Start**, point to **Settings**, and then click **Control Panel**.

2. In Control Panel, double-click **Administrative Tools**.

3. In the Administrative Tools window, double-click **Services.**

Now that you have opened the dialog, find the dbconsole process, which will be written as "OracleDBConsoleORACLE_SID". Look at the Status column for the service to see whether it is Started or Stopped. Double click it to open the Properties page.

In the properties page, ensure that the Startup Type is either Manual or Automatic and not Disabled. Click Start, if the process is not already started. Click OK.

Once the service has been started, open your web browser then type the following URL:

http://hostname:portnumber/em

The installer must have showed the port number on which the OEM is listening. If you have installed Oracle on the localhost and it is running on port 5500, the URL should be as follows:

http://localhost:5500/em

The login page for OEM should be shown. The database should be up and running. Login using a user account that is authorized to access the Database control. You will be taken to the home page of OEM. The performance page of OEM will show how your database is performing.

Other than OEM, you can download and install ASH Viewer and use it to view the performance of your database.

AWR

AWR (Automatic Workload Repository) is a performance gathering and reporting tool in Oracle. The AWR is used to collect performance features such as object usage statistics, wait events for identifying performance problems, ASH statistics etc. The The AWR elapsed-time report (awrrpt.sql)has very valuable information about the health of the Oracle instance. However, considerable skills are required to interpret the results.

To generate an AWR report, you can run the following command:

SQL> @?/rdbms/admin/awrrpt.sql

```
SQL> @?/rdbms/admin/awrrpt.sql

Current Instance
~~~~~~~~~~~~~~~~

   DB Id     DB Name      Inst Num Instance
----------- ------------  -------- ------------
 1483806882 ORCL                 1 orcl

Specify the Report Type
~~~~~~~~~~~~~~~~~~~~~~~~
AWR reports can be generated in the following formats.  Please enter the
name of the format at the prompt.  Default value is 'html'.

'html'          HTML format (default)
'text'          Text format
'active-html'   Includes Performance Hub active report

Enter value for report_type: html

Type Specified:  html
```

Note that you should choose the type of format to display the report in. In my case, I chose "text". You will also be asked to choose the number of days for which you need to generate the report. You should choose the start and end snapshots for the report, as well as the name of the file in which you need to save the report. In my case, I chose the default name which is *awrrpt_1_125_126.txt*.

By default, Oracle generates snapshots once per hour. The purpose of snapshots is to capture statistics, and you may need to manually create snapshots at times different from the automatic capture. This is done using the "CREATE_SNAPSHOT" procedure. Example:

BEGIN

DBMS_WORKLOAD_REPOSITORY.CREATE_SNAPSHOT ();

END;

/

```
SQL> BEGIN
  2      DBMS_WORKLOAD_REPOSITORY.CREATE_SNAPSHOT ();
  3  END;
  4  /

PL/SQL procedure successfully completed.

SQL>
```

The snapshot will be created immediately. To check it as well as the other existing snapshots, just query the DBA_HIST_SNAPSHOT view:

```
SQL> desc DBA_HIST_SNAPSHOT
 Name                                      Null?    Type
 ---------------------------------------   -------- -------------------
 SNAP_ID                                   NOT NULL NUMBER
 DBID                                      NOT NULL NUMBER
 INSTANCE_NUMBER                           NOT NULL NUMBER
 STARTUP_TIME                              NOT NULL TIMESTAMP(3)
 BEGIN_INTERVAL_TIME                       NOT NULL TIMESTAMP(3)
 END_INTERVAL_TIME                         NOT NULL TIMESTAMP(3)
 FLUSH_ELAPSED                                      INTERVAL DAY(5) TO SECOND(1
                                                    )
 SNAP_LEVEL                                         NUMBER
 ERROR_COUNT                                        NUMBER
 SNAP_FLAG                                          NUMBER
 SNAP_TIMEZONE                                      INTERVAL DAY(0) TO SECOND(0
                                                    )
 CON_ID                                             NUMBER

SQL> select snap_id, dbid, startup_time,flush_elapsed snap_level from DBA_HIST_S
NAPSHOT;

   SNAP_ID       DBID
---------- ----------
STARTUP_TIME
------------------------------------------------------------------
SNAP_LEVEL
------------------------------------------------------------------
        88 1489472328
14-DEC-17 08.07.02.000 AM
+00000 00:01:02.7
        93 1489472328
14-DEC-17 08.07.02.000 AM
+00000 00:00:38.6
       103 1489472328
14-DEC-17 08.07.02.000 AM
```

Each snapshot is deleted automatically after 8 days. However, you may need to drop a snapshot manually for the purpose of creating space. This can be done using the DROP_SNAPSHOT_RANGE procedure to drop snapshots whose ids belong to a specified range. Example:

BEGIN

DBMS_WORKLOAD_REPOSITORY.DROP_SNAPSHOT_R ANGE (low_snap_id => 88,

high_snap_id => 120, dbid => 1489472328);

END;

/

```
SQL> BEGIN
  2     DBMS_WORKLOAD_REPOSITORY.DROP_SNAPSHOT_RANGE (low_snap_id => 88,
  3                           high_snap_id => 120, dbid => 1489472328);
  4  END;
  5  /

PL/SQL procedure successfully completed.

SQL>
```

All the snapshots whose IDs range between 88 and 120 will be deleted. Note that you must specify the correct ID of the database (dbid) which you can obtain by querying the DBID field of the DBA_HIST_SNAPSHOT view.

Chapter 9- Oracle SQL Tuning

Indexing

An index is a method of tuning the performance of the database for a faster retrieval of records. An index works by creating an entry for every value contained in an indexed column. Oracle uses indexes to avoid the need for large-table, full-table scans and disk sorts, which are required when the SQL optimizer cannot find an efficient way to service the SQL query.

The following are the types of commonly used indexes in Oracle:

1. Bitmap indexes

    This type of index is well applicable on columns that are not highly selective such as gender. They become more useful when you have many of them on various columns so that they can all be used together to be more selective on rows that otherwise you'd need a full table scan for. It is recommended you use them when you can apply a number of them on various columns. Updates on tables with bitmap indexes are less than efficient.

2. b-tree index

    This is the common type of index in Oracle. After issuing the CREATE INDEX command without further specifications, you create a b-tree index. The b-trees normally store the values of the column you have created the index on, and pointers to the actual table data to find the row itself. They provide a fast access by to an individual row or a range of rows by key, requiring very few reads to find the correct row.

3. Function based indexes

These indexes store the computed result of a function on a row(s), not the column data itself. They allow for creation of indexes on expressions, internal functions, and user-written functions in PL/SQL and Java. Function-based indexes ensure that the Oracle designer is able to use an index for its query. They are created on columns that a function is usually applied on.

When creating indexes, we use the following syntax:

CREATE [UNIQUE] INDEX index_name

ON table_name (column1, column2, ... column_n)

[COMPUTE STATISTICS];

The UNIQUE keyword states that the combination of the values in indexed columns must be unique. The *index_name* is the name to be assigned to the index. The table_name denotes the name of the table for which we are creating the index. The column1, column2, ... column_n are the columns that are to be used in the index. The COMPUTE STATISTICS Parameter tell Oracle to collect statistics when creating the index. The statistics will be used by the optimizer when choosing a "plan of execution" during the execution of SQL statements.

Consider the following example demonstrating how to create an index:

CREATE INDEX student_idx

ON student (name);

```
SQL> CREATE INDEX student_idx
  2      ON student (name);

Index created.

SQL>
```

We have created an index named "student_idx" on the "name" column of "student" table. We could also have created the index on more than one columns of the table as follows:

CREATE INDEX student_idx

ON student (name, age);

Note that you can't create two indexes with the same name on one database. If you run the above command, you will be informed that the index already exists, so the command is only for demonstration purposes.

If we need to collect statistics while creating the index, we could have used the following command:

CREATE INDEX student_idx

ON student (name, age)

COMPUTE STATISTICS;

To rename an index, we use the ALTER INDEX command. The command takes the syntax given below:

ALTER INDEX index_name

RENAME TO new_index_name;

The *index_name* is the name of the index to be changed, while *new_index_name* is the new name of the index. To rename our "student_idx" index to "student_index", we can run the following command:

ALTER INDEX student_idx

RENAME TO student_index;

```
SQL> ALTER INDEX student_idx
  2     RENAME TO student_index;

Index altered.

SQL>
```

The following command demonstrates how we can collect the statistics for a particular index:

ALTER INDEX student_index

 REBUILD COMPUTE STATISTICS;

```
SQL> ALTER INDEX student_index
  2     REBUILD COMPUTE STATISTICS;

Index altered.

SQL>
```

To delete an index, we use the DROP INDEX command that takes the following syntax:

DROP INDEX index_name;

Example:

DROP INDEX student_index;

```
SQL> DROP INDEX student_index;

Index dropped.

SQL>
```

Explain Plan

After passing a SQL statement to Oracle, the CBO (cost based optimizer) uses the database statistics to create an execution plan that it uses to retrieve data in the most efficient manner. The explain plan statement produces the likely execution plan without executing the statement. This is very useful for the case of long-running queries whereby executing the statement may lead to an unacceptable delay to the tuning process. This allows for the display of the execution plan for poorly performing queries without impacting the database.

The information regarding the execution plan is stored in a database which can be created using the utlxplan.sql script script. Login as SYS with SYSDBA privileges then create the table as follows:

SQL> @$ORACLE_HOME/rdbms/admin/utlxplan.sql

If the command doesn't run, it means the plan table had already been created, so you don't have to worry. Make the table available to the public by running the following command:

SQL> GRANT ALL ON sys.plan_table TO public;

```
SQL> GRANT ALL ON sys.plan_table TO public;
Grant succeeded.
SQL>
```

The *autotrace* feature can help us get an execution plan. Once you turn on this feature, the execution plan for all suitable statement runs will be displayed. To turn it on, we run the SET AUTOTRACE ON command as demonstrated below:

```
SQL> SET AUTOTRACE ON
SQL> select * from student;

NAME                          AGE COURSE_NAME
                               20

Execution Plan

Plan hash value: 2356778634

! Id  ! Operation          ! Name    ! Rows  ! Bytes ! Cost (%CPU)! Time     !

!   0 ! SELECT STATEMENT   !         !     1 !     3 !     2  (0)! 00:00:01 !
!   1 !  TABLE ACCESS FULL! STUDENT  !     1 !     3 !     2  (0)! 00:00:01 !

Statistics

         34  recursive calls
          0  db block gets
         42  consistent gets
          0  physical reads
          0  redo size
        681  bytes sent via SQL*Net to client
        552  bytes received via SQL*Net from client
          2  SQL*Net roundtrips to/from client
          3  sorts (memory)
          0  sorts (disk)
          1  rows processed
SQL>
```

That is how you can easily get an execution plan. However, it is inefficient when the query returns several rows. The best way is to run the explain plan statement manually as demonstrated below.

The explain plan statement generates the execution plan for a query without executing the query itself, allowing the execution plan for poorly performing queries to be displayed without impacting the **database. Example:**

EXPLAIN PLAN FOR
SELECT *
FROM student a, course c
WHERE a.course_name = c.course_name
AND a.name = 'JOHN';

```
SQL> EXPLAIN PLAN FOR
  2     SELECT *
  3        FROM    student a, course c
  4        WHERE   a.course_name = c.course_name
  5        AND     a.name  = 'JOHN';
Explained.

SQL>
```

You can then view the plan table by running the following command:

SQL> @$ORACLE_HOME/rdbms/admin/utlxpls.sql

To view the contents of explain.sql file, run the following command:

SQL> @explain.sql

Chapter 10- Oracle Security

RMAN Encryption

If someone steals the database backup you had created with RMAN< it will be possible for them to restore the whole database and steal your data. To avoid this, it is good for you to encrypt the backup. You can query the v$rman_encryption_algorithms view and see the list of encryption algorithms for RMAN.

```
SQL> desc v$rman_encryption_algorithms
 Name                                      Null?    Type
 ---------------------------------------- -------- ----------------
 ALGORITHM_ID                                       NUMBER
 ALGORITHM_NAME                                     VARCHAR2(64)
 ALGORITHM_DESCRIPTION                              VARCHAR2(64)
 IS_DEFAULT                                         VARCHAR2(3)
 RESTORE_ONLY                                       VARCHAR2(3)
 CON_ID                                             NUMBER
SQL> select algorithm_name, algorithm_description,is_default from v$rman_encrypt
ion_algorithms;

ALGORITHM_NAME
-----------------------------------------------------------------
ALGORITHM_DESCRIPTION                                          IS_
----------------------------------------------------------------
AES128
AES 128-bit key                                               YES

AES192
AES 192-bit key                                               NO

AES256
AES 256-bit key                                               NO

SQL>
```

You can see that AES128 is the default encryption algorithm for RMAN. When encrypting the backups, we can use the Oracle Encryption Wallet or password, or even both.

We will be demonstrating how to use a password to encrypt your backup. We can achieve this using the SET ENCRYPTION ON command and setting the password using the IDENTIFIED keyword. Also, add the ONLY keyword at the end of the command in order to state that only password encryption should be used. If this is left, a RMAN Encryption Wallet will be wanted.

First, connect to RMAN from the operating system terminal as follows:

rman target /

Enable encryption by running this command:

RMAN> set encryption on identified by 'Mypassword' only;

```
RMAN> set encryption on identified by 'Mypassword' only;

executing command: SET encryption
using target database control file instead of recovery catalog
```

The encryption has been enabled. Next, backup the USERS tablespace:

RMAN> backup tablespace users;

```
RMAN> backup tablespace users;

Starting backup at 30-DEC-17
using channel ORA_DISK_1
channel ORA_DISK_1: starting full datafile backup set
channel ORA_DISK_1: specifying datafile(s) in backup set
input datafile file number=00006 name=/app/centos/oradata/orcl/users01.dbf
channel ORA_DISK_1: starting piece 1 at 30-DEC-17
channel ORA_DISK_1: finished piece 1 at 30-DEC-17
piece handle=/app/centos/recovery_area/ORCL/backupset/2017_12_30/o1_mf_nnndf_TAG20171230T233026_f4k4jl31_.bkp
  tag=TAG20171230T233026 comment=NONE
channel ORA_DISK_1: backup set complete, elapsed time: 00:00:01
Finished backup at 30-DEC-17

RMAN>
```

Now, try to restore it by running the following command:

RMAN> restore tablespace users;

```
RMAN> restore tablespace users;

Starting restore at 30-DEC-17
using channel ORA_DISK_1

channel ORA_DISK_1: starting datafile backup set restore
channel ORA_DISK_1: specifying datafile(s) to restore from backup set
channel ORA_DISK_1: restoring datafile 00006 to /app/centos/oradata/orcl/users01.dbf
channel ORA_DISK_1: reading from backup piece /app/centos/recovery_area/ORCL/backupset/2017_12_30/o1_mf_nnndf
  TAG20171230T233323_f4k4p3gf_.bkp
RMAN-00571: ===========================================================
RMAN-00569: =============== ERROR MESSAGE STACK FOLLOWS ===============
RMAN-00571: ===========================================================
RMAN-03002: failure of restore command at 12/30/2017 23:34:33
ORA-19870: error while restoring backup piece /app/centos/recovery_area/ORCL/backupset/2017_12_30/o1_mf_nnndf
  TAG20171230T233323_f4k4p3gf_.bkp
ORA-19913: unable to decrypt backup
ORA-28365: wallet is not open
```

This means that if someone had stolen your backup, they will not be able to restore and steal your data, unless they provide the correct password. The restoration can successfully be done by running the following commands:

RMAN> set decryption identified by 'Mypassword';
RMAN> restore tablespace users;

```
RMAN> set decryption identified by 'Mypassword';
executing command: SET decryption
RMAN> restore tablespace users;
Starting restore at 20-DEC-17
using channel ORA_DISK_1
```

If you provide a wrong password, the decryption will not be done.

By default, RMAN uses the AES 128-bit key algorithm for encryption. The algorithm can be easily changed using the CONFIGURE ENCRYPTION ALGORITHM command as follows:

RMAN> show encryption algorithm;

```
RMAN> show encryption algorithm;
RMAN configuration parameters for database with db_unique_name ORCL are:
CONFIGURE ENCRYPTION ALGORITHM 'AES128'; # default
RMAN>
```

RMAN> configure encryption algorithm 'AES256';

```
RMAN> configure encryption algorithm 'AES256';
new RMAN configuration parameters:
CONFIGURE ENCRYPTION ALGORITHM 'AES256';
new RMAN configuration parameters are successfully stored
RMAN>
```

RMAN> show encryption algorithm;

```
RMAN> show encryption algorithm;

RMAN configuration parameters for database with db_unique_name ORCL are:
CONFIGURE ENCRYPTION ALGORITHM 'AES256';

RMAN>
```

If you clear the configuration, the default encryption algorithm will be in use:

RMAN> configure encryption algorithm clear;

```
RMAN> configure encryption algorithm clear;

old RMAN configuration parameters:
CONFIGURE ENCRYPTION ALGORITHM 'AES256';
RMAN configuration parameters are successfully reset to default value

RMAN>
```

To use Oracle Encryption Wallet, we should configure RMAN to perform an encrypted backup of any tablespace or whole database automatically using the CONFIGURE ENCRYPTION FOR command. Example, we will configure RMAN to create encrypted backup of the database, but exclude the users tablespace from encryption:

RMAN> show all;

```
RMAN> show all;

RMAN configuration parameters for database with db_unique_name ORCL are:
CONFIGURE RETENTION POLICY TO REDUNDANCY 1; # default
CONFIGURE BACKUP OPTIMIZATION OFF; # default
CONFIGURE DEFAULT DEVICE TYPE TO DISK; # default
CONFIGURE CONTROLFILE AUTOBACKUP OFF; # default
CONFIGURE CONTROLFILE AUTOBACKUP FORMAT FOR DEVICE TYPE DISK TO '%F'; # default
CONFIGURE DEVICE TYPE DISK PARALLELISM 1 BACKUP TYPE TO BACKUPSET; # default
CONFIGURE DATAFILE BACKUP COPIES FOR DEVICE TYPE DISK TO 1; # default
CONFIGURE ARCHIVELOG BACKUP COPIES FOR DEVICE TYPE DISK TO 1; # default
CONFIGURE MAXSETSIZE TO UNLIMITED; # default
CONFIGURE ENCRYPTION FOR DATABASE OFF; # default
CONFIGURE ENCRYPTION ALGORITHM 'AES128'; # default
CONFIGURE COMPRESSION ALGORITHM 'BASIC' AS OF RELEASE 'DEFAULT' OPTIMIZE FOR LOA
D TRUE ; # default
CONFIGURE RMAN OUTPUT TO KEEP FOR 7 DAYS; # default
CONFIGURE ARCHIVELOG DELETION POLICY TO NONE; # default
CONFIGURE SNAPSHOT CONTROLFILE NAME TO 'G:\APP\NICOH\PRODUCT\12.1.0\DBHOME_1\DAT
ABASE\SNCFORCL.ORA'; # default

RMAN>
```

RMAN> configure encryption for database on;

```
RMAN> configure encryption for database on;

new RMAN configuration parameters:
CONFIGURE ENCRYPTION FOR DATABASE ON;
new RMAN configuration parameters are successfully stored

RMAN>
```

RMAN> configure encryption for tablespace users off;

```
RMAN> configure encryption for tablespace users off;

Tablespace USERS will not be encrypted in future backup sets
new RMAN configuration parameters are successfully stored

RMAN>
```

RMAN> show all;

```
RMAN> show all;

RMAN configuration parameters for database with db_unique_name ORCL are:
CONFIGURE RETENTION POLICY TO REDUNDANCY 1; # default
CONFIGURE BACKUP OPTIMIZATION OFF; # default
CONFIGURE DEFAULT DEVICE TYPE TO DISK; # default
CONFIGURE CONTROLFILE AUTOBACKUP OFF; # default
CONFIGURE CONTROLFILE AUTOBACKUP FORMAT FOR DEVICE TYPE DISK TO '%F'; # default
CONFIGURE DEVICE TYPE DISK PARALLELISM 1 BACKUP TYPE TO BACKUPSET; # default
CONFIGURE DATAFILE BACKUP COPIES FOR DEVICE TYPE DISK TO 1; # default
CONFIGURE ARCHIVELOG BACKUP COPIES FOR DEVICE TYPE DISK TO 1; # default
CONFIGURE MAXSETSIZE TO UNLIMITED; # default
CONFIGURE ENCRYPTION FOR DATABASE ON;
CONFIGURE ENCRYPTION ALGORITHM 'AES128'; # default
CONFIGURE COMPRESSION ALGORITHM 'BASIC' AS OF RELEASE 'DEFAULT' OPTIMIZE FOR LOA
D TRUE ; # default
CONFIGURE RMAN OUTPUT TO KEEP FOR 7 DAYS; # default
CONFIGURE ENCRYPTION FOR TABLESPACE 'USERS' OFF;
CONFIGURE ARCHIVELOG DELETION POLICY TO NONE; # default
CONFIGURE SNAPSHOT CONTROLFILE NAME TO 'G:\APP\NICOH\PRODUCT\12.1.0\DBHOME_1\DAT
ABASE\SNCFORCL.ORA'; # default

RMAN>
```

The configuration can be cleared in order to return to normal by running the following commands:

RMAN> configure encryption for database clear;

RMAN> configure encryption for tablespace users clear;

```
RMAN> configure encryption for database clear;

RMAN configuration parameters are successfully reset to default value

RMAN> configure encryption for tablespace users clear;

Tablespace USERS will default to database encryption configuration
old RMAN configuration parameters are successfully deleted
```

Transparent Data Encryption (TDE)

TDE is a mechanism for encrypting data stored in OS data files. It enables the encryption of data at the storage level to prevent data tempering from outside of the database.

For you to use TDE, you should first create a software keystore. This will act as a container for storing the Transparent Data Encryption key. Its location should be defined in the sqlnet.ora file. To verify whether you have set its correct location in the sqlnet.ora file, query the *v$encryption_wallet* view:

SQL> select * from v$encryption_wallet;

The sqlnet.ora file should have the following parameter specifying the location of the key:

ENCRYPTION_WALLET_LOCATION=

(SOURCE=

(METHOD=FILE)

(METHOD_DATA=

(DIRECTORY=/u00/app/oracle/local/wallet)))

The path for DIRECTORY must match the location you have stored the key.

We can then create the software keystore from the SqlPlus. Ensure that you are logged in as a user with ADMINISTER KEY MANAGEMENT or SYSKM privilege.

SQL> administer key management create keystore '/app/centos/product/12.1.0/dbhome_1/scheduler' identified by manager;

```
SQL> administer key management create keystore '/app/centos/product/12.1.0/dbhome_1/scheduler' identified by manager;
keystore altered.
```

You will notice that the ewallet.p12 will be generated in the location of the keystore. The wallet should now be opened, and if you need to know its status, just query the v$encryption_wallet view. If it is not opened, open it by running the following command:

SQL> administer key management set keystore open identified by manager container = ALL;

You can then activate the key by running this command:

SQL> ADMINISTER KEY MANAGEMENT SET KEY IDENTIFIED BY manager WITH BACKUP;

If you need to create an encrypted tablespace, run the following command:

SQL> CREATE TABLESPACE TEST_ENCRYPTION

datafile '/app/centos/oradata/ORCL/testencry.dbf' size 10M

ENCRYPTION USING 'AES256'

DEFAULT
STORAGE(ENCRYPT);

```
SQL> CREATE TABLESPACE TEST_ENCRYPTION
  2  datafile '/app/centos/oradata/ORCL/testencry.dbf' size 10M
  3  ENCRYPTION USING 'AES256'
  4  DEFAULT STORAGE(ENCRYPT);
```

You can then create a table within that tablespace:

SQL> create table employee_encyption(empno Number(3), Name varchar(10)) tablespace TEST_ENCRY;

You can query the dba_tablespaces view to see whether the table has been created and encrypted:

SQL> select tablespace_name,encrypted from dba_tablespaces where tablespace_name='TEST_ENCRY';

The following command can help you create a table with an encrypted column , Salary:

SQL> CREATE TABLE employee (

FirstName VARCHAR2(128),

LastName VARCHAR2(128),

EmpID NUMBER,

Salary NUMBER(6) ENCRYPT

);

Data Redaction

The data redaction feature was first introduced in Oracle 12c, and it allows for the masking of sensitive data from the end-user layer. Before the Oracle 12c, one had to create views to "hide" sensitive column but in 12c, you can use the data redaction feature. A good example of data redaction is the use of asterisks when writing sensitive information such as password. Oracle Data Redaction enables you to mask (redact) data that is returned from queries issued by applications. The following are the various types of redaction:

1. Full redaction- redacts all of the contents of the column data.

2. Partial redaction- redacts a portion of the column data.

3. Regular expressions- use regular expressions to search for patterns of data to redact. Example, you can use regular expressions to redact email addresses, which may have

different character lengths. It is designed for use with character data only.

4. Random redaction- The redacted data presented to querying application user is displayed as randomly generated values every time it is displayed, depending on column data type.

5. No redaction- This type option enables you to test the internal operation of redaction policies, with no effect on the results of queries against tables with policies defined on them.

For you to be able to add a redact policy, you should have the execute privileges on DBMS_REDACT package.

```
SQL> grant execute on DBMS_REDACT to HR;

Grant succeeded.
```

Note that redaction policies will NOT be supported when you are connected as SYS and when you have the EXEMPT REDACTION POLICY system privilege. The Redact policy can be created as follows:

BEGIN

DBMS_REDACT.ADD_POLICY (

object_schema => 'SCOTT',

object_name => 'EMP',

column_name => 'SOCIAL_SECURITY_NUMBER',

policy_name => 'REDACT_CARD_POLICY',

function_type => DBMS_REDACT.FULL,

expression => '1=1'

);

END;

/

The expression "1=1" will always evaluate to a true, hence the column "social_security_number" will always be redacted for the user Scott.

User Accounts

In Oracle, you can create two types of user accounts:

1. Common User- A common user is created in root Container DB. Common user can connect to root CDB and all Pluggable DB's including future Pluggable DB's which you may plug.

2. Local User- A local user is created in a PDB database and he can connect and has privileges in that PDB only.

Use the following command to create a common user account:

SQL> create user user1 identified by User1Password;

```
SQL> create user user1 identified by User1Password;
User created.
SQL>
```

The user will have the name "user1" and his password will be "User1Password". For you to run the above command, you must be connected with Sysdba privileges. If you try to connect to the database as usera, you will get an error:

```
SQL> connect user1/User1Password
ERROR:
ORA-01045: user USER1 lacks CREATE SESSION privilege; logon denied

Warning: You are no longer connected to ORACLE.
```

This is because the user has not been granted the "connect" privilege. Grant the user privileges by running the following command:

SQL> grant connect, resource to user1;

```
SQL> grant connect,resource to user1
  2  ;

Grant succeeded.
```

After that, we will be able to connect to the database using user1 account:

```
SQL> connect user1/User1Password
Connected.
SQL>
```

If you need to lock a particular user's account, meaning that they won't be able to log into their account, run the following command:

SQL> alter user username account lock;

Example:

SQL> alter user user1 account lock;

```
SQL> alter user user1 account lock;

User altered.

SQL>
```

Again, you must be connected with Sysdba privileges. Try to login as the user and you will get an error:

```
SQL> connect user1/User1Password
ERROR:
ORA-28000: the account is locked


Warning: You are no longer connected to ORACLE.
SQL>
```

To unlock the user account, you only have to replace the "lock" with "unlock".

```
SQL> connect sys as sysdba
Enter password:
Connected.
SQL> alter user user1 account unlock;

User altered.

SQL> connect user1/User1Password
Connected.
SQL>
```

To create a new password, use the ALTER USER command as follows:

SQL> ALTER USER user1 IDENTIFIED BY mypassword;

```
SQL> ALTER USER user1 IDENTIFIED BY mypassword;

User altered.

SQL>
```

The above should be done once an account expires as you can only revive it by assigning a new password. To delete a user account, use the DROP USER command:

SQL> DROP USER user1;

```
SQL> DROP USER user1;

User dropped.

SQL>
```

If the user had created objects in the database that you also want to delete, add the CASCADE clause to the end of the command:

SQL> DROP USER user1 CASCADE;

Roles

It may be difficult for one to administer large numbers of objects.

Oracle roles allow you to localize the administration of objects. Oracle roles are most helpful when large numbers of users will need the same system and object privileges. An Oracle role is created using the CREATE ROLE command. The Oracle role can then be granted to users and all the privileges will be transferred along with that grant. Roles can help reduce the number of grants for security purposes.

A role can be identified globally by using the GLOBALLY keyword in the IDENTIFIED clause. This means the role will be authenticated by the Oracle Security Server.

The following command demonstrates how to create a role in Oracle:

SQL> CREATE ROLE clerk IDENTIFIED by clerkpass;

```
SQL> CREATE ROLE clerk IDENTIFIED  by clerkpass;
Role created.
SQL>
```

The role can then be granted privileges to the various tables as follows:

SQL> Grant select on COUNTRIES to clerk;

```
SQL> Grant select on COUNTRIES to clerk;

Grant succeeded.
```

After that, we can make one of the users in the database a clerk by granting them the role of the clerk as follows:

SQL> GRANT clerk TO OE;

```
SQL> GRANT clerk TO OE;

Grant succeeded.
```

This means that user account OE will be able to do whatever a clerk can do.

To revoke the role of a clerk from Nicholas, we should run the following command:

SQL> REVOKE clerk FROM OE;

```
SQL> REVOKE clerk FROM OE;

Revoke succeeded.
```

To drop a role, we use the DROP ROLE command as follows:

```
SQL> DROP ROLE clerk;
Role dropped.
SQL>
```

Profiles

You can create limits on system resources that are under use by setting up profiles with some defined limits on the resources. Profiles are useful in large and complex organizations with many users. They allow one to regulate the amount of resources that are used by each database user by creating and assigning the profiles to users.

A profile can be created using the CREATE PROFILE command. The command takes the following syntax:

>---CREATE PROFILE profile LIMIT
resource_parameters|password_parameters--;->
Resource_parameters (you can specify multiple paramters per

command):
[SESSIONS_PER_USER n|UNLIMITED|DEFAULT]
[CPU_PER_SESSION n|UNLIMITED|DEFAULT]
[CPU_PER_CALL n|UNLIMITED|DEFAULT]
[CONNECT_TIME n|UNLIMITED|DEFAULT]
[IDLE_TIME n|UNLIMITED|DEFAULT]
[LOGICAL_READS_PER_SESSION
n|UNLIMITED|DEFAULT]
 [LOGICAL_READS_PER_CALL
n|UNLIMITED|DEFAULT]
[COMPOSITE_LIMIT n|UNLIMITED|DEFAULT]
[PRIVATE_SGA n [K|M]|UNLIMITED|DEFAULT]
Password_parameters (Oracle8 and above):
[FAILED_LOGIN_ATTEMPTS
expr|UNLIMITED|DEFAULT]
[PASSWORD_LIFE_TIME expr|UNLIMITED|DEFAULT]
[PASSWORD_REUSE_TIME expr|UNLIMITED|DEFAULT]
[PASSWORD_REUSE_MAX expr|UNLIMITED|DEFAULT]
[PASSWORD_LOCK_TIME expr|UNLIMITED|DEFAULT]
[PASSWORD_GRACE_TIME expr|UNLIMITED|DEFAULT]
[PASSWORD_VERIFY_FUNCTION
function_name|NULL|DEFAULT]

Example:

CREATE PROFILE profile1

LIMIT PASSWORD_REUSE_MAX 10

PASSWORD_REUSE_TIME 30;

```
SQL> CREATE PROFILE profile1
  2     LIMIT PASSWORD_REUSE_MAX 10
  3            PASSWORD_REUSE_TIME 30;

Profile created.

SQL>
```

Notice we have used the PASSWORD_REUSE_TIME and PASSWORD_REUSE_MAX parameters. The PASSWORD_REUSE_TIME parameter defines the number of days before which a password cannot be reused. The PASSWORD_REUSE_MAX defines the number of password changes needed before the current password can be reused. You can also set the following password parameters:

- PASSWORD_LOCK_TIME - defines the number of days an account will be locked after the specified number of consecutive failed login attempts.

- PASSWORD_GRACE_TIME- defines the number of days after which the grace period begins during which a warning will be issued and login is allowed. If the password is not changed during the grace period, the password expires.

- PASSWORD_VERIFY_FUNCTION- this clause lets a PL/SQL password complexity verification script be passed in the form of an argument to CREATE PROFILE statement. The Oracle Database usually provides a default script, but one can create their own routine or use a third-party software instead.

CREATE PROFILE profile2 LIMIT

SESSIONS_PER_USER UNLIMITED

CPU_PER_SESSION UNLIMITED

CPU_PER_CALL 3000

CONNECT_TIME 45

LOGICAL_READS_PER_SESSION DEFAULT

LOGICAL_READS_PER_CALL 1000

PRIVATE_SGA 15K

COMPOSITE_LIMIT 5000000;

```
SQL> CREATE PROFILE profile2 LIMIT
  2        SESSIONS_PER_USER           UNLIMITED
  3        CPU_PER_SESSION             UNLIMITED
  4        CPU_PER_CALL                3000
  5        CONNECT_TIME                45
  6        LOGICAL_READS_PER_SESSION   DEFAULT
  7        LOGICAL_READS_PER_CALL      1000
  8        PRIVATE_SGA                 15K
  9        COMPOSITE_LIMIT             5000000;
Profile created.

SQL>
```

The following is an example of a profile with the password limit values set:

CREATE PROFILE profile3 LIMIT

FAILED_LOGIN_ATTEMPTS 5

PASSWORD_LIFE_TIME 60

PASSWORD_REUSE_TIME 60

PASSWORD_REUSE_MAX 5

PASSWORD_LOCK_TIME 1/24

PASSWORD_GRACE_TIME 10;

```
SQL> CREATE PROFILE profile3 LIMIT
  2        FAILED_LOGIN_ATTEMPTS 5
  3        PASSWORD_LIFE_TIME 60
  4        PASSWORD_REUSE_TIME 60
  5        PASSWORD_REUSE_MAX 5
  6        PASSWORD_LOCK_TIME 1/24
  7        PASSWORD_GRACE_TIME 10;
Profile created.

SQL>
```

You can assign a user to a particular profile by use of the ALTER

USER command. Example:

SQL> ALTER USER HR PROFILE profile2;

```
SQL> ALTER USER Nicholas PROFILE profile2;
User altered.
SQL>
```

To modify a profile, use the ALTER PROFILE command.

ALTER PROFILE profile2 LIMIT
FAILED_LOGIN_ATTEMPTS 2;

```
SQL> ALTER PROFILE profile2 LIMIT FAILED_LOGIN_ATTEMPTS 2;
Profile altered.
SQL>
```

To delete a profile, use the DROP PROFILE command as follows:

```
SQL> DROP PROFILE profile1;
Profile dropped.
SQL>
```

Chapter 11- Oracle Clustering

Oracle Clustering

The goal of Grid computing is to provide high availability information sharing that is supported by an architecture having sufficient resource allocation in such a way that the users can rely on getting as much information or processing as they need on demand. Users no longer have to consider where their data is being stored or where their data request are processed because the database grid is supported by RAC (Real Application Clusters) and Oracle Clusterware and the storage grid is supported by the Automatic Storage Management (ASM) system.

The Oracle Grid Infrastructure manages Oracle cluster-related functions such as membership, group services, global resource management, and databases. Oracle Grid Infrastructure is required for every Oracle RAC instance. The Oracle Grid Infrastructure is made up of the following components:

- A cluster interconnect responsible for allowing cluster communications

- A private virtual IP address responsible for cluster communications over the interconnect

- A public virtual IP address responsible for client connections

- A public IP address as a Single Client Access Name (SCAN) address on the Domain Name Server (DNS) for round robin resolution to three IP addresses or at least one IP address

- Shared storage accessible by each node

Data Guard

Oracle Data Guard ensures there is a high availability, data protection, and disaster recovery for enterprise data. It provides a set of services that can be used to create, maintain, manage, and monitor one or more standby databases to enable production Oracle databases to survive disasters and data corruptions. The Oracle Data Guard keeps these standby databases in the form of copies of the production database. Then, if the production database becomes unavailable because of a planned or an unplanned outage, Oracle Data Guard can switch any standby database to the production role, minimizing the downtime associated with the outage.

Oracle Data Guard may be used with the traditional backup, restoration, and cluster techniques in order to provide a high level of data protection and data availability. Oracle Data Guard transport services are used by other Oracle features like Oracle Streams and Oracle GoldenGate for an efficient and reliable transmission of the redo logs from a source database to one or more remote destinations.

An Oracle Data Guard configuration is made up of one production database, also known as the *primary database* that works in the primary role. This is the database accessed by most of the applications.

A standby database is a transactionally consistent copy of a primary database. By use of a backup copy of the primary database, one can create up to thirty standby databases then incorporate them into Oracle Data Guard configuration. Once created, the Oracle Data Guard automatically keeps every standby database by transmitting the redo data from primary database and applying the redo to standby database.

Note that Oracle Data Guard is available only as a feature of the *Oracle Database Enterprise Edition*. The feature is not available in the *Oracle Database Standard Edition.*

RMAN Catalog

The RMAN recovery catalog is a schema that is stored in a database and it is responsible for tracking backups and storing scripts to be used in RMAN backup. For most all backup operations, you will want to connect to both the database and the backup recovery catalog, using the "catalog" option.

The enrolling of a database in a recovery catalog for RMAN use is called *registration.* The recommended practice is to register each target database in your environment in a single recovery catalog.

RMAN can only connect to a single instance in Oracle Real Application Clusters database at a time. Assume that targt1, targt2, and targt3 are net service names for three instances in an Oracle Real Application Clusters configuration. In such a case, you can only connect to the target database using only one of the net service names. Example, you can connect as follows:

% rman TARGET SYS/Syspassword@targt2 CATALOG rman/Rmanpassword@orcl

Every net service name should specify one and only one instance. You can't specify a net service name that uses Oracle Net features to distribute connections to more than one instance.

Chapter 12- Oracle DBA

Tasks

When working as an Oracle Database Administrator (DBA), you can be involved in the following tasks:

- Installing Oracle software

- Creating the Oracle databases

- Starting up and shutting down the Oracle database

- Managing the storage structures of the database.

- Performing upgrades of databases and software to the new release levels

- Managing users and security

- Making the database backups and performing recovery whenever necessary

- Managing schema objects like tables, indexes, and views

- Monitoring and tuning performance of the database

- Proactively monitoring the health of the database and taking preventive or corrective action as needed.

In a small or midsize database environment, the DBA might be the sole person performing the above tasks. In large, enterprise environments, the job is usually divided amongst several DBAs, each with their own specialty, like database security or database tuning.

Responsibilities

The following are the responsibilities of an Oracle DBA:

- Performs the capacity planning required to create and maintain the databases.

- Performs ongoing tuning of the database instances.

- Controls migrations of database changes, programs, reference data changes and menu changes throughout the development life cycle.

- Implements and enforces security for all the Oracle Databases.

- Performs database re-organization as needed to assist performance and ensure there is maximum uptime of the database.

- Puts standards in order to ensure that all the application design and code is produced with the necessary integrity, security and performance. The DBA performs reviews on design and code frequently to ensure site standards are adhered to.

- Evaluates the releases of Oracle as well as its tools, and third party products to ensure the site is running products that are appropriate.

- Manages the sharing of resources amongst the applications.

- Creates new database users as needed.

- Troubleshoots any problems regarding the databases, applications and the development tools.

References

1. https://docs.oracle.com/cd/B28359_01/server.111/b28318/part_2.htm

2. https://becomeadba.com/2008/05/24/basic-oracle-architecture/

3. http://www.datadisk.co.uk/html_docs/oracle/structure.htm

4. https://docs.oracle.com/cd/B19306_01/server.102/b14220/intro.htm

5. http://www.dba-oracle.com/concepts/rman_online_offline_backups.htm

6. http://www.thegeekstuff.com/2013/08/oracle-rman-backup/

7. http://www.datadisk.co.uk/html_docs/oracle/asm.htm

8. http://www.dbatoolz.com/t/tkprof-when-and-how-to-use-it.html

9. https://intellipaat.com/tutorial/oracle-dba-tutorial/database-backup-restore-and-recovery

10. http://www.dba-oracle.com/art_sql_tune.htm

11. https://www.theregister.co.uk/2014/05/06/oracle_database_performance_workshop/

12. http://www.dataintegration.ninja/32-tips-for-oracle-sql-query-writing-and-performance-tuning/

13. https://docs.oracle.com/cd/B28359_01/network.111/b28531/intro.htm

14. http://www.dba-oracle.com/grid_cluster_definition.htm

15. http://www.dba-oracle.com/t_job_duties.htm

16. https://www.dbametrix.com/responsibilities-dba.html

www.ingramcontent.com/pod-product-compliance
Lightning Source LLC
LaVergne TN
LVHW052308060326
832902LV00021B/3768